Working Dogs

Sled Dogs

by Kimberly M. Hutmacher

Consulting Editor: Gail Saunders-Smith, PhD

Consultant: Jane Fuerstenau
Secretary, Mush with PRIDE
Fairbanks, Alaska

CAPSTONE PRESS
a capstone imprint

Pebble Plus is published by Capstone Press,
151 Good Counsel Drive, P.O. Box 669, Mankato, Minnesota 56002.
www.capstonepub.com

Books published by Capstone Press are manufactured with paper
containing at least 10 percent post-consumer waste.

Library of Congress Cataloging-in-Publication Data
Hutmacher, Kimberly.
    Sled dogs / by Kimberly M. Hutmacher.
    p. cm.—(Pebble plus. Working dogs)
    Includes bibliographical references and index.
    Summary: "Simple text and full-color photos illustrate the traits, training, and duties of sled dogs"—Provided by
publisher.
    ISBN 978-1-4296-4472-3 (library binding)
    1. Sled dogs—Juvenile literature. I. Title. II. Series.
SF428.7.H88 2011
636.73—dc22   2009051416

Editorial Credits
Erika Shores, editor; Bobbie Nuytten, designer; Marcie Spence, media researcher; Eric Manske, production specialist

Photo Credits
Capstone Studio/Karon Dubke, cover (collar)
Dreamstime/Ventura69, 15
fotolia/El Gaucho, 21
iStockphoto/benoitrousseau, 9 (top); s5iztok, 5
Marilyn Trump, 17
Shutter Point/Jeffrey Gresio, 7
Shutterstock/Bart Goossens, 13; Glen Gaffney, 19; Marcel Jancovic, 11; Nagy Melinda, 9 (bottom left);
    Sirko Hartmann, cover, 1, 9 (bottom right)

Note to Parents and Teachers

The Working Dogs series supports national social studies standards related to people, places, and culture. This book describes and illustrates sled dogs. The images support early readers in understanding the text. The repetition of words and phrases helps early readers learn new words. This book also introduces early readers to subject-specific vocabulary words, which are defined in the Glossary section. Early readers may need assistance to read some words and to use the Table of Contents, Glossary, Read More, Internet Sites, and Index sections of the book.

Printed in the United States of America in North Mankato, Minnesota.
102010
005987R

Table of Contents

Snow Dogs

Sled dogs go to work
when it's cold outside.
They pull sleds over ice
and snow.

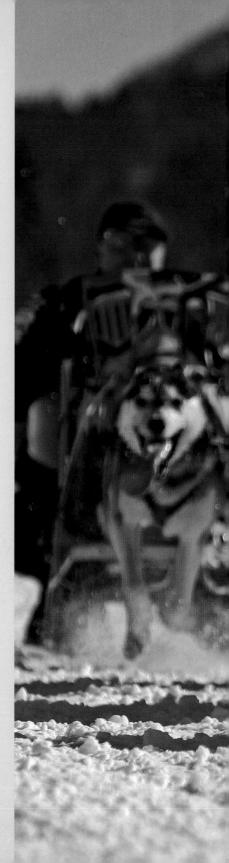

Sled dogs compete in races.

Up to 20 dogs are on a team.

The Iditarod is a popular race

across Alaska.

A Good Sled Dog

Most sled dogs are
Alaskan huskies, Siberian
huskies, or Alaskan malamutes.
They are strong and fast.

Alaskan huskies

Siberian huskies

Alaskan malamutes

9

Sled dogs have thick fur

to keep warm.

Thick skin on their paw pads

keeps them from slipping

on ice and snow.

Sled dogs are smart
and friendly.
They get along well
with other dogs.

Training a Sled Dog

Mushers lead sled dog teams.

Dogs and a musher learn

to work together.

From birth, sled dogs train,

eat, and play together.

Puppies learn to wear
a harness to pull. They pull
small loads short distances.
Adult dogs pull heavy loads
long distances.

Sled dogs learn commands.

Mushers yell "hike" to go.

They shout "whoa" to stop.

Sled dogs train all year.

When snow falls, these dogs

are ready to race!

Glossary

command—an order to follow a direction

compete—to try hard to outdo others
at a race or contest

harness—a set of straps and metal pieces
that attach a dog to a sled

Iditarod—a famous dog sled race; dogs run
more than 1,000 miles (1,600 kilometers)
from Anchorage to Nome, Alaska

musher—the person who drives a team
of sled dogs

Read More

Haskins, Lori. *Sled Dogs.* Dog Heroes. New York: Bearport Publishing, 2006.

Whitelaw, Ian. *Snow Dogs! Racers of the North.* DK Readers. New York: Dorling Kindersley, 2008.

Internet Sites

FactHound offers a safe, fun way to find Internet sites related to this book. All of the sites on FactHound have been researched by our staff.

Here's all you do:

Visit *www.facthound.com*

FactHound will fetch the best sites for you!

Index

Word Count: 159
Grade: 1
Early-Intervention Level: 15